After Twenty-five Years of Smoking Crack, How You Like Me Now

Gregory Mack Thomas

Order this book online at www.trafford.com
or email orders@trafford.com

Most Trafford titles are also available at major online book retailers.

Printed in Victoria, BC, Canada.

ISBN: 978-1-4269-3360-8 (soft)
ISBN: 978-1-4269-3361-5 (ebook)

*Our mission is to efficiently provide the world's finest, most comprehensive book publishing
service, enabling every author to experience success. To find out how to publish your book, your
way, and have it available worldwide, visit us online at www.trafford.com*

Trafford rev. 8/11/2010

 www.trafford.com

North America & international
toll-free: 1 888 232 4444 (USA & Canada)
phone: 250 383 6864 ♦ fax: 812 355 4082

Acknowledgements

I would like to thank God first and foremost for his unconditional love and bringing me through all my trials and tribulations. Also for loving me when I didn't lov3e myself. I would also like to thank my mentor John Hamilton "aka" Majestic for helping me to become the better man that I am today. For teaching me all about the Lord Jesus Christ while serving time in the Federal Prison. Thank you Majestic for your time, patience, love and knowledge may our father keep you blessed. I would like to thank Michael Green for being there when I needed him; he wrote all my letters for me to family and friends because I couldn't, Big thanks Michael. I would never forget what you done for me, God Bless you. I would like

to thank my dearest grandmother Flossie Mack without her being in my life this book would not be possible. Also like to thank Jose Canas, James Neal, Lisa Davis and my cousins Loretta and Abul.

My father Robert, Debbie Edens, Sharon Turman, Charles Perry, and Taiquan Unique thank you all for helping me get this book published. Also would like to thank Lionel Lefevre, MD and his secretary Delores. Thank you to my parole officer Tanya Parris, my sentencing federal judge Sterling Johnson for being patient with me. I also would like to thank the love of my life Vanessa Mitchell.

Special Thanks

Thank you Teddy for helping me get my grandmother out of the nursing home and for teaching me everything I needed to know to take care of her and I am still taking care of her to this day. I would like to thank you for helping me; you'll like a brother to me. Thank you; love always.

To Benny Cook

The only man I've known to be my father. Thank you for teaching me how to be a man.

Dedication

I would like to dedicate this book to my dearest grandmother Flossie Mack, who has struggled all her life to maintain keeping the family together. While I was on drugs she continued to give me unconditional love and prayed for my recovery.

My grandmother and I is all the family we have left. In spite of some family members and friends. She out lived all four of her children (My mother and three uncles) who are all deceased. She has two grand children that are also deceased (Derek Mack, my brother and a cousin Pookie Mack). My grand mother out lived most of her family she's now 90 years of age as this book is being written. She's been there for me through out my life and my incarceration. I vowed to God to take care of her and to return the unconditional love and commitment that she has given to me. At times it can be very difficult taking care of her because she suffers from dementia so I dedicate this book to my dear loving nana.

Chapter 1

The day it all began at the age of fourteen, when I stated smoking weed. This became my gateway to hell and ultimately it led me to the belly of the beast. In time you will comprehend where the belly of the beast is.

Marty and I was smoking weed in the building of 1569 Prospect Place when the police rolled up on us and tried to bust us for a nickel bag of weed. When I resisted arrest the police beat my ass then took me to the 77th precinct and beat my ass some more than they let me go. At the time the police officers names were Batman and Robin, who became my archenemies every time Batman and Robin would see me they would stop me to harass me, smacking me around going in my pockets illegally. Their abuse and their harassment caused me and most of my friends to dislike white police officers.

At the age of sixteen in 1974 Marty and I were playing hooky from school getting high then we decided to go to Prospect Park as we normally do. We got on the Franking Avenue shuttle train then we ran into a bunch of Tomahawks gang members. Marty and I were surrounded by at least fifteen gang members they asked us what gang were we in so naturally we said the tomahawks from Brownsville. Then the leader of the gang told Marty and me that we were hanging with them. We were not gonna argue with fifteen gang members so we went with them. We winded up going back to Brownsville by the way of the A train. The Tomahawks started walking through the cars of the train Marty and I followed them. As we were approaching Utica Avenue on the A train we came upon two white females. Then the gang members started touching them between their legs, then the girls started screaming. At this time the train came to a complete stop at Utica Avenue and it wasn't moving. Police officers started coming and running from every direction, the train doors had opened up. Marty and I had separated our selves from the gang members then headed for the nearest exit. When one police officer was coming down the stairs as we were going up he grabbed Marty and me. Marty being bigger and stronger than me he was able to snatch away from the police officer without me knowing his intentions that caused the officer to grab me with both hands. I tried to fight the officer off me but I was too lite in the ass to get away.

Both of the girls on the train pointed me out then said that I sexually assaulted them, which led me to Riker's Island for the first time in my life for one month. I was scared as hell at that time because they had a homosexual in jail by the name of mother (Madea) who was a booty bandit taken ass left and right, and I was not trying to give up on ass. I came home one month later on

November 8, 1974 the case was dismissed because of lack of evidence because the accusers said I was the shortest one in the crowd so she picked me. My lawyer said bullshit is that the reason why you pointed my client out she said yes and then the judge dismissed the case. For the record I would like it to be known that I did not take the pussy I'm not a rapist. I have plenty of women that will love to fuck me at the drop of a dime. But I only have one good one that I love and she gives me all the lovin that I need and then some. After the sexual assault was dismissed, two months later while getting high off weed one late night me and Marty with several other friends were hanging out in front of the court building 1569 Prospect Place minding our business when all of a sudden out of nowhere cops rolled up on us and we started to run but a friend of mines by the name of Koko said don't run we didn't do anything so we stay there then the cops pulled out their guns on us the bastards then said get against the wall, you fuckin nigga so we did I said what did we do? The cop said shut the fuck up you fuckin nigga you know what the fuck you did you broke into the cleaners on the corner. I said no we did not So did my friends and everyone else said no we wouldn't do no bullshit like that they said that was some bullshit then all of a sudden two more police cars pulled up out of nowhere because it was a dark foggy night so we couldn't see them coming. They also pulled their guns on us pulled out their handcuffs then they cuffed us, Me, Koko, Hatchet, and once again Marty managed to slip away into the fog, they put us in the police cars smacked us up as they normally do kick our asses, spit in our face, and beat our asses some more then took us to the 77th. Precinct. Then the next thing I knew we were on our way downtown to central booking for arraignment. Now for the second time in my life I was on my way back to Riker's Island. This time when I got to the Island I went to a place called C76. My friend Koko I have no idea where he was because he was doing the jail shit way before I was, when I got to C76 I had a pair of Pro Keds Sixty-niners with the stripes on the side then some guy came to my cell with a shank. He had muscles ten times the size of Arnold Schnagger, he told me when my cell opens up to pass my sneakers to him or else he's going to stab my ass the nigga was big as hell, shit he didn't need no shank. He had muscles on top of muscles my little punk ass was glad to pass those sneakers. So as soon as the cell opened up I passed him those sneakers then he passed me some bullshit raggedy ass Skippy's sneakers as time went on a week had passed I was tight with the big muscle bond mother fucker an I was no longer a new jack. After being in jail with him we became friends, he gave me my sneakers back. Then new jacks started coming in then I started taking their sneakers. Two days after that I went to court I was offered one year in jail or five years probation. Now you tell me readers, which one do you think I took? Yes, I took the year no just kidding I took the five years probation with my punk ass I wasn't trying to do a week moreless a year.

My friend Koko said come on man do this year with me, you could so this I got your back. But remember now Koko had been jailing long before I met him. I was still a scared little punk waiting for the opportunity to get out so when my lawyer said what do you want to do? I raised my hand fast as hell and said, please give me the five years probation then they did then Koko said to me, yo, Greg you are going to regret that and he was right. When I got out Koko was still in jail doing a year and before his year was up I got arrested again like he said I did regret being on probation.

I was arrested for Robbery and Assault on a seventy-two year old white man. I went to court once again; Marty and Hatchet were part of this crime with me. Marty was sentenced to a year, and the system wanted to give me seven years because I was on five years probation prior to my arrest and then two years for this new case which added to seven years altogether. I went to court with Marty and his lawyer, his lawyer decided to separate our cases with that I got scared. So as court went into recess I left the court building. At that time my mother worked in the welfare center at Flatbush Avenue downtown Brooklyn. I went to my mother's job I told my mother what happened in court and what they were trying to do which is give me seven years and that I was running from the law. My mother said, son are you sure that's what you want to do? My scary ass said hell yeah ma I can't do no seven years with all those booty bandits in jail. She asked where are you going? Do you have any money? Then I said yes I saved some money and I'm still getting money and I don't know where I'm gonna go but I know I'm not going back to Riker's Island. So my mother said son I love you I know you know what you're doing cause you're a smart young man. You do what you have to. I'm not going to talk you out of it because I'll be wasting my time you know what you're doing. I looked at her then started crying. She kissed me on my forehead then she grabbed my face on both sides kissed me on my nose, told me she loved me and to be careful. I grabbed her and hugged her then told her not to worry that I'll be alright then I left. I then went to my grandmothers house told her what happened in court and that I'm now on the run a fugitive. As crazy as it may seem I always wanted to be a fugitive. Because I watched the television series called the Fugitive so I am now the character that I wanted to become David Jensen. I got into more trouble me, Hatchet, and of cause Marty. This time around we robbed a white man we got four dollars from the white man so they told me and a black and white TV then we sold the TV for twenty-five dollars. Everybody in the neighborhood saw us robbed this white man. While on the corner of Prospect and Ralph Avenue we went up in his apartment like we had a license to rob the white man but me, I stayed downstairs, I was the lookout man while Marty and Hatchet went upstairs. I don't know what was going on upstairs but I heard screaming and hollering then the next thing I know they were coming downstairs with a TV. In broad daylight we were running down the street with a TV. The law abiding citizens in the neighborhood couldn't stand our thieving asses. They were tired of our shit so someone called the police on us. They knew where to find us but they didn't catch us until about a month later. They caught Hatchet first, Marty second, and me they had a hard time catching me cause by then I was a fast little motherfucker and I use to dress up like a woman.

Chapter 2

Now that I'm a fugitive I need a place to hide. I then stay at my grandmother's house decking and hiding from the police. I stayed at my grandmother's house throughout the winter for six months on the run. Decking the police scared as hell because some people knew that I was on the run that I didn't want to know. I knew that one of them would rat me out. The in editable happened, one day while laying in my grandmothers' apartment at 184 Monroe Street in Brooklyn, one of my uncles had stolen some money that I gave my grandmother. I was asleep on the couch that particular day when I heard my grandmother crying and it woke me up. I asked my grandmother why she was crying. She said someone had stolen the money you gave me. I asked her, did they take all of it? She said yes. That made me very angry cause there were only three people in the house, my two uncles, my grandmother, and myself. I said to my grandmother don't worry because whoever took it is going to give it back. I then went to my uncles and asked them who took my grandmothers money. Naturally they both said they didn't take it. I threaten to kick both their asses if they didn't give my grandmother back her money by the time I wake back up. I went back to sleep when all of a sudden the sounds of walkie-talkies woke me up. To my surprise one of my uncles had called the police on me. They also told them that I was a fugitive. Then a police officer standing over me tapped me with his night stick he asked me is your name Gregory Mack

Thomas? Then I said, yes. The officer said, I heard that you are a fugitive. I said, no I'm not you have the wrong person. The officer said to me, get up let's go down to the precinct and straighten this out. I asked him who told you that? Then the officer said, one of the gentlemen in the kitchen pertaining to my two uncles in the kitchen. I then said to the officer, check one of them in the kitchen, ask them are they fugitives giving myself time to think the matter through. What will be my next move? Then the officer called back up in the living room to watch me while he himself goes into the kitchen to interrogate my uncles. At that time I said to the officer that was watching me, let me put on my pants and sneakers. He said go ahead as I was putting my pants on I looked towards the window and saw that it was closed. My grandmother lived on the second floor. I had to make a choice whether I wanted to go to jail or escape and remain on the run. The choice was simple I chose freedom. I put on my wife beater with my jeans and my sneakers. I looked out the window then looked at the officer and I made a fifty-yard dash to the window then dived through the window as if I was diving in a pool now me being a gymnast, I tucked and rolled then landed on my feet when I hit the pavement.

There was three feet of snow outside so I slipped as I was landing then literally landed on my ass and was knocked out for a couple of seconds. When I woke up face up the police were looking out the window yelling that crazy nigga dove through the window. Then I got up realizing that I was in my grandmother's backyard and I had a chance to get away. So I started running through the snow ass hurting from the pain, I also had a cut on my shoulder from diving through the window. I came to the front of the building I peeped out to see if there were any police out there. I realized they were all upstairs. So I ran down Monroe Street like a bat out of hell. There was no way that they were gonna catch me cause I was a fast little mother fucker so I ran across Nostrand Avenue down towards Marcy Avenue when I came across an abandon building, I went up to the second floor shaking, shivering and bleeding profusely from my shoulder. I saw a dirty curtain hanging from the empty apartment I snatched the curtain wrapped it around my shivering body then I backed up in corner to get my thoughts together, realizing that I was bleeding badly and that my bloodstains were in the snow leading to where I was at. Then I knew I had to get the fuck out that building before my bloodstains lead the police to me. I came out the building ran two blocks into a restaurant looking crazy as hell. I came across two black women in the restaurant. Then one of them asked me little boy are you alright? I said, no I'm bleeding, so the lady went into the back of the restaurant then come back with a wet towel. She wiped the blood from my cut while trying to stop the bleeding but it wouldn't stop bleeding cause the cut was too deep. At that time I wanted to leave because I thought the cops would find me there because of my blood trail.

Then the lady asked, is there anything else I can do for you? I said, yes can I make a phone call to call my mother? She said, yes but I never called my mother I called Marty's mother who's like a mother to me. I told her what had happened and that I needed some help. She told me to catch a cab come to her house and she would take care of me. I took a cab to her house then her daughter Jewel met me on the corner of Prospect and Buffalo Avenue with a wig, a dress, high heel shoes, and lipstick. She paid the cab then got in with me then dressed me up as a woman.

She then walked me to the building of 1569 Prospect place. The reason she dressed me as a woman because a lot of people in the area knew that I was a fugitive and were jealous. They also would like to see me go to prison because I was a menace to society so they thought. Jewel thought it was best I dress up like a woman so no one would notice me as we walked to her building. As we were walking towards her building I noticed that there were a lot of people in front of the building. Some friends and foes but none of them recognized me when I walked passed to Marty's mother apartment. I walked into the apartment in extreme pain then Marty and his twin sister Tina helped me into Marty bedroom. Where they helped me take off my clothes, got hot water pads to put on my lower back then they cleaned me up and fed me something to eat. They took care of me for about two weeks before I got better, Marty mom asked me what I was going to do. Then I said I don't know. She said you could stay at Phyllis house she lives in Flatbush. After I got better I went to stay at Phyllis house. I stayed with Phyllis cleaning and watching her kids while she worked. When she gets off work I would leave then go out to snatch pocket books. I snatched pocketbooks for a living and let me tell you I was very good at it too. I snatched pocketbooks for about six months. The money that I would get I would take it to my grandmother to let her hold it. Every time that I would bring her money she thought that I hit the numbers. Until one day I snatched a pocketbook around Avenue D and got caught. The police arrested me beat my ass as usual cause I had a smart mouth but they let me go. The woman's pocketbook that I snatched she didn't' like that at all so she called the newspaper to have the Judge disbarred. I didn't know I was at Phyllis house chilling when all of a sudden Phyllis mom called Phyllis and told her that she's reading the New York Daily news and that my picture is in the paper with a story about me and the lady whose pocketbook that I snatched. That she's dissatisfied with the results of my case. She wants the Judge to answer why he let my go without knowing who I really was and that she had three thousand dollars in her purse.

Marty mom told me to go downstairs to get the newspaper and read the article. I went to get the paper came upstairs then looked through the paper to find the article cause at that time I couldn't' read so it was difficult for me to read the story. I asked Phyllis, Marty's' sister to read it to me. She read the story and when she finished reading I thought to myself, man, I got to get the fuck out of dodge. I'm already a fugitive and now this so I talked to Marty's mom; she said to me she has some people in California and that I can go out there to stay. So I went to my grandmother's house got all my money, which accumulated to three thousand dollars and fifty-two cents. I got on the plane to go to California to live with some people that I didn't even know. But they accepted me as a family member. I used an alias name, which was Derek. My adopted cousins looked after me.

Chapter 3

When I got off the plane my adopted cousins were not at the airport so I had no idea where I was going I caught a cab to Pico and Wilton Place. The cab driver charged me fifty dollars from L. A. airport to Wilton Place; well later on I realized that he ripped me off big time. When I got to 1408 Wilton Place I got out the cab with my two suitcases went upstairs to the second floor my now cousin Kathy let me in the house, when I got inside the apartment the place was filled with people and it was 3am in the morning. I had no idea where I was or who the hell was all these people. I was in the house filled with strange people in a strange city. Alone and scared but I knew I couldn't go back to New York. I had to dig deep down inside myself and bring out the tuff New York attitude so I did. I trusted no one because I'm a New Yorker. So me not trusting anyone made it hard for me to live with these strangers. I had about ten different people that were a couple of years older than me trying to tell me what to do and how to live in Los Angles. Remember now I was a thief, a liar, and a con artist. In my eyes these people were slow so I don't know what the fuck made them think that I was going to listen to their slow Asses. After all I'm a motherfuckin New Yorker and so as time went on I learned that I had to humble myself if I wanted to stay with these people and not get caught because let's not forget I'm still a fugitive.

So I began to listen to these people in order for me to survive in Los Angeles and not to go back to jail in New York. As time went on I got closer to my new found cousins because they helped me find myself and in the process of finding myself I began to like myself and others. I also began to meet interesting people I met people I couldn't dream of meeting. My cousin father God bless his soul noticed that I couldn't read or write. He took the time and patience to help me, but I wasn't ready to read or write hell I'm in a strange city and in my eyes they were fresh meat after all I'm a liar, a thief, and a con artist s o I had to exercise my talents and I did. I snatched pocketbooks like nobody's business in Los Angeles. Them motherfuckers didn't know what hit them in Los Angeles you either had to have a car or a bike I didn't know how to drive but I knew how to steal. So I stole the best-got dam bike money could buy and it was called the Swim, after, all I was surrounded by the motherfuckin rich and I do mean rich. They had pools in every backyard, orange trees all over the streets I mean if I was thirsty, all I had to do was reach over in somebody's fence and thee was an orange waiting for me. I begin to love this place I wasn't getting no pussy. I didn't have a girlfriend but I had the best clothes my theivin ass could get. I mean these motherfuckers were so innocent and naive they left the best shit on the clotheslines. I was like a little boy in a candy factory. Whatever I wanted to wear I just took it off some bodies clothesline. Whatever I wanted to eat I just reached in their got dam yard. California was the shit to a New Yorker like myself, and I took full advantage of it. Remember now these mother fuckers were slow the cops were pushovers the streets were so empty at times I thought I was on a different planet. So whenever I didn't have money I would get on my brand new swin bike and ride around looking for victims to rob. My bike made it so easy because they didn't have pocketbook snatchers such as myself in a city such as this. So I stepped up my pocketbook snatching game I would park my bike right on the victim street then leave it there with no chain on it, I would sneak up behind the bitch while she's going in her apartment building wait until she gets to her floor while creeping up behind her let her take her keys out put them in the lock then bam! Out of nowhere here I come they never knew what the fuck hit them by the time they turned around they couldn't describe what I looked like whether I was black, white or Chinese because they never saw me coming got dam it for that matter or leaving. When I had the pocketbook, as I'm running down the stair I would pull out a shopping bag put the pocketbook in the bag then walk out of the building just as calm walk over to my bike and slowly ride away until I get to the next corner. Once I get to the corner then turn I rode that bike like a bat out of hell, in my case a New Yorker running from the police.

Then I perfected my art every time I snatched a pocketbook. I got so good at this shit until it became a job to me. I mean I would literally get up everyday as if I had a job to go to and snatch pocketbooks. My cousins they had no idea until this day they thought that I was selling clothes cause I had found a wholesale place that I could buy shirts and hats to sell on the streets or at least make them believe that I was selling clothes on the street. Little did they know that when I took my bike and bag of clothes out that I had a spot where I would hide my clothes? Then I would ride around looking for victims and if you think that I was successful in snatching pocketbook in New York hell, I was a millionaire in California and I never got caught.

One day Kathy told me she had a job interview for me. She was a summer youth counselor at a place called Say Yes. She told me to go to this particular building actually it was a bank how ironic. When I arrived at the bank I met the manager she interviewed me then asked me if I knew how to file. I had no idea what the fuck she was talking about but I said yes. After all I'm a liar remember if you don't I do. After the interview the manager said that she would notify my cousin Kathy in a couple of days. So I went home told my cousin what happened with the interview and that the manager will notify her in a couple of days. Then I went back to snatching pocketbooks. About two days later Kathy calls me one morning while I was on my way to work snatching pocketbooks she told me to go to the bank to start work the manager is going to hire me. I was nervous, as hell after all I have never been around business people before more less work with them but I went. When I got there I met the manager she showed me around and told me what she wanted me to do. She introduced me to the other employees and this was very awkward for me after all I'm a thief, a liar and a con artist a wanted man dressed up in a white shirt and tie. I mean where the fuck is the puma sneakers, the kango hat, and the jeans. I didn't see any of that all I saw was a bunch of suits and money all around me. My ghetto instincts wanted to rob their asses but I had to remember that I'm a fugitive and that my cousins reputation and good name was on the line so I snapped out of that thinking and did what the manager asked me to do which was putting files in alphabetical order and to my surprise I was good at it but I hated that shit. I did it for one week thinking that I was finished when I left that Friday I said goodbye to the people that I met at the bank as if I would never see them again. I was shaking hands with men and women but I was shaking their hands faking a smile I looked at them then said to myself you just don't know motherfucker how lucky you are with that gold watch on; you have no idea whose hand you're shaking. They had some good ass jewelry on them too one of them had on a watch that I knew was worth a couple of thousands. Now I realize that he had on a got dam Rolex watch. Not knowing that I would be coming back to the bank next week I went home saw my cousin Kathy, she told me that the manager and the employees at the bank likes me and that I done an excellent job. That made me feel good it was a feeling of euphoria that come over me that I never felt. Then I asked myself why me? I don't deserve to be here. Why do these people like me? I'm nobody but they did like me. Then I found myself asking myself many of times why me, because doors of blessings which I didn't understand that they were blessings were opening up to me. I didn't know God. I didn't even know his son Jesus. I didn't even know the devil but they all knew me. And all of them used me whenever they need me I guess I didn't mind I wasn't in jail I was around people that loved me and showed me how to love back. So my life took a turn for the better. I started thinking like a Californian instead of a New Yorker I started caring these feelings that I never had in New York about people were coming out of me in California I mean the people that I would rob in New York with no hesitation would let me into their house and feed me and would leave me alone with thousands of dollars right in front of me and I couldn't understand it so again I asked a question to this entity called God, why me? I got no answer if I did get the answer I didn't know it was an answer. So I accepted everything that come my way the blessings and the curses. The curses were many my cousin Peter got me another job working in a condominium in Beverly Hills. It was called Sierra Towers. I was working there as a bell hopper to my surprise a lot of celebrities lived in this building. It was the tallest building on the sunset strip right on the borderline of Hollywood Boulevard in Beverly Hills. When I started working there I met celebrities such as: Ray Parker Jr., who I became a close friend with, Jack Webb, Producer of Dragnet and Adam 12, Steve Martin, and several other well-known celebrities. In this building is where all the curses began. I started meeting people who had connections to cocaine.

Chapter 4

As, I started chauffeuring these people around to different restaurants like the Cock-N- Bull and the Magnet. I started going inside to pick up my clients. When I arrived inside these various restaurants I noticed that my clients weren't ready to leave at the schedule time so they would tell me to have a seat and a drink. Then the next thing I knew a gram of cocaine would appear out of nowhere I would be sitting around millionaires wondering to myself what the fuck am I doing here sitting with these millionaires drinking Bacardi and coke, but that's not what they called it the name of this drink was called Acuber libra. These guys would sit and talk about millions of dollars right in front of me and would include me into their conversations as if I knew what the fuck they were talking about they get so drunk and coked up they started asking me questions like Derek, what do you think of me investing in this particular product? Then I would sit there with the dumbest look on my face and I'll answer hey do what you have to do you've been doing good so far you must be doing something right all of a sudden a gram of cocaine would come my way then the drinks, me being honored to be around millionaires. I would accept the drugs and the drinks as if it was a badge little did I know that it was leading up to something more cenacle than I could ever imagine that would be freebasing. Something that, I didn't know anything about that was mention while sitting around these rich clients that I use to chauffeur. One of them had asked me Derek, what the fuck is freebasing? I said I have no idea but I will find out. That conversation had come up when Richard Pryor had made the news when he burned himself freebasing. That evening after the conversation about freebasing I drove one of my clients home then I went home with that question on my mind. I was determined to find out what it was I figure by me knowing that would score brownie points for me so when I got home I asked a friend of mine who lives upstairs in the apartment building where I lived what is freebasing? He said to me its cocaine mixed with baking soda. Then he said to me I could show you better than I can tell you. Then I said ok tomorrow when I get off work come to my house and I'll have some cocaine and baking soda waiting. I asked him what else will I need then he said a small mayo jar, a rubberband, a stocking cap, a bottle of 151 Bacardi rum, acottonball, and a hangar. So the next day when I got home from work he came to my apartment then started putting all these ingredients together while I was standing by him watching snorting my cocaine and smoking my cocaine cigarette. It made me feel like I was on top of the world I thought I was the motherfuckin man cause I had connections to the best shit a poor man could have I had that rich man's cocaine cause I fucked with the rich people. I didn't have to snort the ghetto shit and my friends knew that the cocaine that I had was better than theirs like I said my cocaine came from the rich motherfuckers that I was chauffeuring. While he was cooking this cocaine it had jelled up as I watched the cocaine and the baking soda connected into one rock then he took the mayonnaise jar out of the pot of boiling water and put a cube of ice into the mayonnaise jar, then started shaking it around as I watched it turn into a solid white rock. He then poured the rock onto the stocking cap draining the residue then he took the rock off the stocking cap with a razor blade then he put it into a glass bubble pipe as I watched in amazement. As he scraped the residue from the razor blade on to this glass pipe and it was a lot of residue then he took one of the cotton balls wrapped it around a hangar then dipped the cotton ball onto the 151 Bacardi Rum. Then I asked him what the fuck is you doing? Dipping that shit in the rum I thought that was for us to drink that's, that good shit that ain't that cheap ass Bacardi that we normally drink then he said to me calm down we could still drink this its just to make a torch 151 Bacardi rum burns better than rubbing alcohol. I still didn't know what the fuck he was talking about because I have never seen anyone smoke crack before so I said to myself ok calm down Derek and learn something so he lit this cotton ball with a Bic lighter, than he put it to the glass bubble pipe and all I could hear was a sizzling sound and shit popping then I watched as smoke came from the top of that pipe traveling down into his mouth then when it reached into his throat I watched him because like I said I had never seen no shit like that before so So I wanted to see what the fuck it was gonna do to him I noticed his jaws swollen up as he reached out to pass the glass pipe to me. He was stuck on stupid because I was asking him how do you feel? And he couldn't answer me he started sobbing from the mouth and I'm still asking him how do you feel? Then I said yo, Aaron, are you alright? Still I got no answer he had the stupidest look on his face and at the same time he was scaring my ass, so I just backed up as he stood in my kitchen sobbing and trying to get his composure together then I just watched in absolute amazement then after about ten minutes had passed by he started trying to talk his words were slurry I could see that he was still stuck on stupid and what I mean by that is the cocaine rock still had full control of his body functions. Then after about another three to four minutes had passed his words had become clearer and the sobbing had slowed down then he started comprehending my words once again. I asked him yo, nigga are you alright? He then said yeah that's some good shit. Keep in mind now that the motherfucker had my cocaine not that cheap ghetto shit that he use to smoking. So I could only imagine that the shit he had in his system was forming a whole new brain in his got dam head and at the same time popping some motherfuckin blood vessels in his head cause all he could say was Dam! This is some good shit and where did you get it from? I told him don't worry about where I got it from. Do you like it? The answer was self-explanatory then he passed the pipe to me. So I said to him I'm not smoking this shit the way you just smoked it. Just give me a little bit because that shit had you looking retarded so I took the pipe in my hand then I dipped the cotton ball into a separate glass of Bacardi 151 rum because I wasn't fuckin up Bacardi with no dam cotton ball that shit was too expensive. So I dipped my cotton ball into the rum then I lit it with full control of how I pulled on this glass dick. Then I inhaled one small breath not to take in as much as he did then I quickly blew that shit out in fear of looking retarded like him and slobbing not knowing what the fuck it was gonna do to me. Hell he was use to that shit but not me, and he was not use to the good cocaine that I had. So when I inhaled and blew out the smoke he asked, How do I feel? Then I said to him, man! That shit didn't do nothing to me. I'm not wasting my motherfuckin cocaine on this shit. This shit aint doing nothing for me then he said to me, you blew it out too quick you have to hold it longer and inhale it. Try it again then I said ok I'm gonna try it one more time and if this shit don't do anything this time you can take that shit and get the fuck out my house. So I inhaled again I shouldn't have done that because that shit went straight through my body and long and behold there I was like him stuck on stupid slobbing from the mouth I had no control over my body functions not only was I slobbing from the mouth I had pissed on myself and I almost shitted on myself but he saw that I was stuck on stupid and that it was my first time, so he kept grabbing and shaking me then he went to my refrigerator to get some milk and told me to drink it as he was talking to me and shaking me asking me are you alright? All I could do was just look at him with that same stupid ass look that I saw on his face I'm quite sure that it was on mine, but more intense. Then slowly but surely I started comprehending what he was saying to me and all I could hear is, are you alright? It was at a time when I could hear him but I couldn't understand shit he was saying. I would look at him and see his lips moving and all I could hear is rubbish that to me didn't make any sense finally it added up to are you alright? My dumb ass said yeah lets do that shit again wow! Is this what Richard Pryor burned himself on? How the fuck did he do that? Then I said to my friend teach me how to cook this shit up and he did. At least I thought I knew how to cook this shit because I wanted to smoke this shit by myself. So I watched him cook up another rock gave him half then I put his ass the fuck out cause I had more cocaine then him and I wasn't about to let him smoke up all my shit.

Chapter 5

After he left my apartment I thought I knew how to cook this shit up so I mixed the ingredients together thinking that I was doing it the way he showed me but I had no idea what the fuck I was doing instead of me putting water in the mayonnaise jar along with baking soda and cocaine my non-experience dumb ass put Bacardi 151 rum in the mayonnaise jar with cocaine and baking soda. Now somebody tell me, where the fuck is the water? Than I put the top on the mayonnaise jar to seal all this shit here then I said to myself yeah! Now I know how to do this shit then I dipped the cotton ball in the 151 rum took a pull off the pipe that I had already with freebase in it put a match to the torch put the torch to the mayonnaise jar shaking this shit around and that shit blew up in my dam face, cocaine all over the place scared the shit out of me but do you think that I stopped there not me. I went and got my friend again told him to show me how to do this shit again step by step. I told him what I did then I asked him what went wrong? He said to me you stupid ass you lucky you didn't lose your eyes. You wasn't suppose to put rum, cocaine, and baking soda together you was suppose to use water in the jar. Then I said oh shit! No wonder the shit blew up in my face. So I put the ingredients together in front of him the right way while he coach me through it and long and behold I became a expert at cooking up freebase in that one day. The next day I went to work I saw some of the clients that I chauffeured around who asked me what is freebase then I explained to them what it was and just as I was amazed at the development of how this drug was formed I explained it to them. One of them out of the crowd called me to the side and asked me could I show him how to cook up this cocaine if he supplies the coke and the women we'll have a party at a motel. I had to bring the ingredients which were eight pipes, two mayonnaise jars, three pints of 151 Bacardi Rum, a box of cotton balls, and six wire hangars that he gave me the money for. I got off work that evening at 5:30pm went home took a shower, changed my clothes went to the various stores to get the necessities that I needed at 7pm my client came in a big Mercedes Benz and three white women in the car with him to where I live at 1408 Wilton Place. I went downstairs I thought I was the motherfuckin man being picked up in a big ass four-door sedan Mercedes with three white women. I got in the car we went to a motel on Sunset Blvd. He had the room reserved for us already. We went to Pioneer Chicken to get some food then went straight to the motel. Once we arrived at the motel we went into our reserved room I cooked up the cocaine to last for a week, I showed him how to cook it as he asked me to and that's when the party begins. Each of us had a pipe; a piece in one pipe there was a rock that was big as ten cent. Remember we were using the kind of pipes that had a bubble. We started pulling on our pipes as I'm pulling on mine; I was peeping out the corner of my eye at everyone and watching how they are inhaling these drugs. My friend the guy that I was with was greedy he was inhaling too fast as I watched him the women were being dainty with their pulls but like I said my friend was being so fuckin greedy he inhaled so much at once until his ass fell out. He took a pull and I saw his eyes rolled to the back of his head as I continued to pull on my pipe. I looked at his ass in amazement as I started to choke off my shit, as I watched his head hit the floor it was as if someone punched him in his jaw and knocked him the fuck out. The shit was so good the women got scared and rushed over to his aid but me I just kept right on fuckin pulling on my shit because I knew that this was some good fuckin cocaine and I was not going to let that motherfucker blow my shit. I said to myself them bitches got him I looked at him and saw that he was starting to come around so I kept on fuckin pulling on my crack pipe because I realized that I had some good shit up in this pipe this was not that cheap ghetto shit. This was some celebrity Hollywood Beverly Hills shit here. I treated my pipe with the utmost respect so when I realized that the motherfuckers was alright I asked him, do you want some more? And he said, yes. I tried to tell him with my eyes lit up like the sun I mean I was beamed the fuck up and then I said to him, you have to take it easy man, you can't be pulling on this shit like you pulling on a joint take your time motherfucker your new at this shit don't you know that this shit will stop your fuckin heart as I struggled with myself to get the words out of my mouth I mean I was so high that it took me dam near thirty minutes to get two words out of my mouth. When I finally got my composure together I asked him was he alright. He said, yes then I told him do not put so much in the pipe at the same time cause he don't know what the fuck he's doing and the shit is good stop being so fuckin greedy so I went over to him and helped him put some in the pipe I then lit it for him and I showed him how to pull it slowly he listened then everything was ok then we started focusing on the pussy. I told the girls to go in the bathroom to take showers. As I watched them undress I started getting a limp hard on as I'm trying to focus on the women getting undress I pulled my dick out and started rubbing and playing with it to get it up but it wouldn't rise like I wanted it to as any crack head knows at least back in the 80's when the shit first came out you take a pull of that shit and your dick was not trying to get hard it was not rising your mind wanted the pussy, but your body was not having it so I asked one of the girls to give me some head to get it up a little more an then she started sucking it but the dick still refused to get hard its like the dick wanted more crack it seems like the dick was asking me where the real pussy at? You know you have to put her in the pipe. So the girls started walking to the shower and I followed them with my dick out and the pipe in my hand puffing on the pipe looking crazy as a motherfucker as I walked passed a mirror and saw myself I finally ended up in the bathroom with the girls I sat on the toilet and I watched them wash their selves and kiss like the two lesbians that they were. As they washed I sat there with the pipe in one hand and my dick in the other jerking it off then I got up got a face cloth put soap on it and then I started washing the girls thinking that I could get a arousal out of that but once again my dick reminded me that that's not the pussy it wanted so I stepped back from the girls put some crack in my pipe and I gave my dick the pussy it wanted I took a crazy pull this time shit started poppin all up in my head. I started hearing bells in shit and if you think my ass couldn't talk for thirty minutes on the first hit man, you should have seen what this one did to my black ass. I was two seconds from doing what my friend did and by that I mean passing the fuck out but the but the pipe reminded me that it was still there because my dumb ass took that mega blast that I told you about and I forgot that I put the pipe in my socks by my ankle out of being paranoid then all of a sudden when I thought I was gonna pass out my skin starting burning from the pipe because the glass was so hot it burned me so bad that my skin started to peel off but that didn't stop me I got me some Vaseline and toilet paper put it on my ankle and rolled my socks back up. I used my sock as if it was a band-aid then I got my ass up off the toilet walked back in the room where everyone else was at still, numb and dumb founded I walked over to the girls that were naked and I started eating one of their pussy. Now as I'm trying to eat her pussy my mind is not on the pussy I mean I'm licking her pussy and looking all over the room not focusing on her pussy because the cocaine wouldn't let me, my eyes and my mind was all over the room and I could hear her say don't stop! Don't stop! And then I found myself telling her to please be quiet while I try to focus in on what the fuck is going on around me because I was so paranoid and eating her pussy was the last thing on my mind so for about a hour I stayed between her legs trying to eat her pussy, but I couldn't so I finally got up off my knees and walked to the refrigerator, then opened a Heineken and started drinking it. Then I noticed my thoughts coming back I mean that cocaine was some good powerful shit this white boy had the kind that I knew that I had to respect so I did. I sat around watched the girls and my friend freaking off with each other then I went and got a joint then started smoking it. Then I noticed my dick starting getting hard while I was watching them, then I thought to myself dam! My dick is getting hard let me go over there and let one of them bitches suck my dick then I did. She started sucking my dick and I was getting harder and harder now I was ready to eat some pussy and fuck but I had to eat the pussy first because that's my shit so I started eating her pussy like the champ that I knew I was about to become today.

Chapter 6

Spending so much time with these women I found myself so tired, with all the food we had I barely ate food. I was too busy eating pussy and freebasing. The same shit day and night fuckin, smoking and eating pussy but not eating enough food but loving every minute of that shit I mean I thought I was the motherfickin man with two white freaky bitches, plenty of cocaine, alcohol, and weed. I mean what more can a motherfucker ask for but I knew eventually this shit would have to come to and end either the drugs would run out or this shit would kill me which ever came first I really didn't give a fuck. Then after about six days in this hotel I knew my cousins were worried about me so I had to end this shit on the seventh day. So I smoked less cocaine that day and a lot more pussy eating and fucking but after I came for the last time I got dress and didn't even wash my ass kissed the girls then shook my man hand and left their asses right up in there before these motherfuckers kill me with these goddam drugs. I got on the bus on Sunset Boulevard rode the bus to Western Avenue in Hollywood transferred to another bus got on that bus and rode to Venice Boulevard walked four blocks to my home. On my way about two blocks from my house I ran into a neighborhood drug dealer who asked me where have you been. I haven't seen you in a couple of days do you need anything? Because I got that good shit! This shit is pumping. Then I said to him hell no I'm good so he went his way and I went into my building.

As I was going upstairs I saw one of my female cousins and she asked me are you alright? I said yes why, she said because you look different. I asked her what do you mean by that. She said nothing you just look tired and sleepy. I said nah I'm good then I went in the apartment went straight to the bathroom in the bathroom the lighting was brighter than it was in the motel so I could see myself a lot clearer and when I looked into the mirror I saw what my cousin didn't want to tell me that she saw. I realized that she lied to me about how bad I looked. I mean I looked like pure death, but I just didn't want to lie down. When I looked into that mirror I said oh shit! You could see my cheekbones, my eyebrow bones, my lip bones and we know that we don't have lip bones, but got dam it I did. I mean my skin was dark I got four shades darker and at that moment I realized that I was a base head, but in New York I would have been known as a crack head it was then and there when I said to myself that I'm going to stop but that was not the part that scared the shit out of me the part that scared the shit out of me was when I took off my clothes to take a shower I could literally see my rib cage and able to count how many I had. I could also see my heart pumping looking like it was coming through my chest at that point I looked down and saw that my dick had shirked to the size of my dam pinky finger, I mean I had a dick before I just smoked it off.

Again I made the decision to stop getting high but as we know its not that easy the shit sounds good but hard to do. So I at least made the decision to stop for one week and there was no such program such as NA (narcotics Anonymous) at least not to my knowledge, the phrase NA sometimes known as never alone, which is a very good program to help drug addicts. So after that week was up I went back on the run and found myself in deeper shit chasing the drugs. What I mean by deeper shit is that I started selling my clothes, my wife items, such as her wedding band and sneaking shit out of the house lying to her and stealing from our kids, also not paying bills such as rent until it got to the point where my family and I was evicted from our apartment fortunately my wife had a brother and a sister who lived in the same building that we were evicted from. So her brother allowed my wife and kids to live with him and his wife, but not me. I had to sleep in my car. I hadn't hit rock bottom yet, but I was really hurting my family as well as myself by my drug addiction. What I mean by hurting my family is that my wife had to put up with a lot of shit from her brother and sister- in-law a lot of verbal abuse came from her brother about me, but my wife stayed with him while I continued to sleep in my car and go to work. She also worked too so we had the chance to save up some money between the both of us while I continued to work. Whenever I got paid I would give my money to my wife for about six months because I knew that if I kept my money that it was what we call today a trigger which back then I had no knowledge of the power of my addiction so as long as I continue to give my wife my money I knew that it was in good hands and we saved up enough within the course of six months. I believe we had about three thousand dollars, which we had accumulated to move into another apartment. But at that time we were not ready we were trying to save more money yet we were still looking at apartments. We looked at several and were undecided of which one to move into. But as fate has it my brother in-law forced my hand to the point where we had to move in sooner than expected. Why? Because one day when I came home from work and parked my car where I normally park it which is right outside the window to where my wife and kids were staying that particular day as I was getting out of my car my wife must've heard me pulling up and looked out the window and saw me little to my surprise before I could barely get to her window to tap on it to let her know that I'm home if you wanna call living in my fuckin car which I did to myself home then so be it. She met me outside as I started walking towards her I noticed that she had tears in her eyes with my daughter Chanelle on her right hip. So I ran over to her and I asked her what's wrong? Then she told me in these words that her brother had pushed her and was saying all sorts of negative things to her about me, and the condition that we were living in and that it was my fault. I couldn't get mad at him, because he was right but he had crossed the line when he put his hands on my wife. I mean that's his sister and obviously he knew her long before I did but nevertheless she's still my wife. Now mind you now even though I was freebasing because at that time it was not called crack but I was still into my martial arts and I thought that I was Bruce Lee son. Furthermore his sister was no longer a Williams. But she was a Mack better yet she was a Thomas and you don't put your hands on a Thomas without repercussions behind that shit. After she told me what happened I went and knocked on his door of cause I was mad as hell because he had pushed her with my daughter in her hands. He opened the door looked at me then I said come out I want to talk to you for a second. He noticed the look in my face and he saw that I was very upset. Looked in his face and I noticed the fear in his face then I asked him what the fuck is your problem man? I told him don't put your motherfuckin hands on my wife. She told me you pushed her if you have a problem with her come see me. At that time my name was Derek, which is my deceased brothers' name, which is the name that I used because I was on the run from the law in New York. Everyone knew me in Los Angeles as Derek even my wife called me Derek. Now getting back on track my brother in-law said to me Derek I didn't push her you know I wouldn't do that wither having Chanelle in her arms. Then my wife said to me he's lying, yes he did with tears coming down her eyes. I knew that he didn't stand a chance against me and that he was her brother I didn't want to fuck him up so it was easier for my wife and I to just get in the car and go to a motel until it was time for us to move into our new apartment. As time went on we finally moved in our apartment about a month later. Things were going just fine at that point. I realized that we could not go down that path again, so I did everything within my power even though I was still on drugs. To make sure that my wife and daughter would not be homeless again. As time went on I got worse with my addiction but I had some money coming in at that time, I had a lawsuit.

My addiction was so powerful to the point where I couldn't understand why I was doing the things that I was doing. I started stealing from my family again I also found myself going in and out of what the call in Los Angeles the county jail. My family that I had in California before I met my wife Margaret which were the people that I called my family until this day who helped me when I needed them the have not heard from me for quite sometime like about a year, because I didn't want them to see me in such a state of mind. Like I said the drugs had me so fucked up til where my wife decided that she had enough of my shit and she wasn't going to put up with it anymore so she put me out in the street. But that didn't stop me from fuckin up my life some more and everyone who came in contact with me. I was dying and liked it I just wasn't dying quick enough this is how sick and distorted my thinking was; I have gave up on life. Some how God didn't give up on me at that time I didn't know why I had begged God to please let me die if it is the only thing I'm here for is to freebase. I felt so all-alone, despite the many so-called friends that I had around me getting high with me and fucking me as long as I had money. But as we know when the money runs out so does the pussy and the so-called friends but I managed to bounce back and find more friends and pussy. I just couldn't find the strength to stop freebasing and hurting my family, but my wife still loved me and my game was so good at least I thought it was to where she took me back which was a big mistake on her behalf. Because I fucked her life up some more I had the attitude of a thief, a liar, and a con artist. I just couldn't stop hurting the people that loved me, so once again my wife put my ass out but before she did she sold the car we had. We were suppose to split the money and go our separate ways her going back to New Jersey to her mother and father and me going back to New York to my dear sweet loving grandmother, Flossie who had been there for me all my life. She was a blessing that I couldn't see at that time. Now let's get back to my wife and this money we were suppose to split for this car well my wife sold the car but she didn't give me half of the money. She gave me some of the money. I think she sold it for a thousand or two but she only gave me one hundred dollars, which made my sick ass angry as hell. She also brought two plane tickets, which I didn't know about one for her, and one for me. Now when I got that hundred dollars I went right to the crackhouse got my crack and got me two strawberries which in L.A. was another name for skiers, which is another name for hoes, dick suckers, sluts then we went to a motel and fucked and sucked and smoked and ate all the pussy that my nasty ass could eat since I learned how to eat pussy. When that was over I went back to my wife apartment begging for some more money, but she wouldn't give it to me. So like the drug addict that I was I act a dam fool and started tearing up the housed looking for money, which made her call the police on my dumb ass but I didn't give a fuck. I told her call the fuckin police hell them the motherfuckers that got my crack anyway much shit they took from me and while you callin them tell them to bring some of that shit with them.

So I sat my ass down and I waited for them to come, but my wife didn't know at the time that I had found her wedding ring so I ran out the back door and went to the pawn shop got sixty dollars for that ring brought me some more freebase come back in the door that I left out from, snuck my ass in the closet that she never go in and started smoking my ass off. All of a sudden I could hear walkie-talkies and they were getting louder. Margaret had so much clothes in this particular closet I buried myself underneath them. When the cops open the door they didn't even see me then they closed the door back and started walking back into the living room so I realized now I could sneak out the back door again so that's what I started to do. I started to take the clothes off of me and opened the door slowly. Long and behold who was standing there looking at me my little cute little smart ass daughter Chanelle. She started hollowing out daddy, mommy there go daddy while one of my legs was still stuck under these clothes. I'm telling her Chanelle be quiet, shut up, but she wouldn't stop by then the police was on my ass. Like I said my left leg was still stuck in the clothes so there was no need for them to tell me to get my ass on the floor because I was already there. Then one of the cops put his knee in my back while the other cop put handcuffs on me. I was so weak from fuckin and smoking crack all day I couldn't even fight back while they were cuffing me all I could hear was my daughter Chanelle saying mommy look at daddy look mommy the police they got daddy mommy, look at daddy.

As they escorted my ass out the house and then to the neighborhood precinct, but it didn't stop there see because they put me in a cell by myself with a phone so I called Margaret ass all nite, until the crack wore off my ass or she got tired and took the phone off the hook which ever came first but none of that shit happened because she called the precinct and told them that I was calling her so they took me out that cell and put me in one without a phone. But being a New Yorker I cursed them motherfuckin cops out see to m e back then in the earlier 80's the cops were soft in Los Angeles, I felt like they didn't have shit on me I'm a New Yorker and I acted like one until the bitter end, but I cursed them motherfuckers out until I got tired and called myself going to sleep. The crack started wearing off my ass so I wanted to go to sleep, but that's not what the cops had in mind. See they waited for my ass to go to sleep because they didn't know exactly what I was high off of freebasing or PCP, because all that shit was fairly new to them and in L.A..

A person high off of PCP had the strength of twenty men and yes I smoked some of that shit to so they waited but I didn't know that they were waiting for a reason for me to go to sleep. Then all of a sudden they came in there with flashlights and started beating my ass. They also knew that Margaret had brought me a plane ticket and that she was leaving the next day to go back to New Jersey and that she wasn't pressing charges. So they had fun kicking my ass and I cried like a little bitch not because of the ass whooping but because reality had set in and I realized that I had lost my family all because of drugs and that I might not see them again and you know what? I was right, Til this day I have not seen my wife or one of my daughters, but let's get back to the precinct the next morning when I woke up I asked the cops when I'm going to court? One of the cops said to m e you're not we're letting you go in a couple of hours your wife is gone; she's back in New Jersey. She brought you a plane ticket and left it with her friend Melody.

Chapter 7

I got out of jail the next day went to my house and there was a note on the closet door telling me where the plane ticket was and that her and my children had left and went to New Jersey. So I got my things together the last of my clothes, called Melody then she came to pick me up and took me back to her house were as she surprised me by pulling out some crack. Now mind you I didn't know that Melody smoked crack even though all the years that I known her. Come to find out she wanted to fuck me along time ago better yet suck my dick.

So we started smoking the crack then she started giving me some head and we continued for about five hours smoking and her giving me head until we ran out the next day then she tried to get more I think she got about two more dimes so we smoked that then she tried to get more on credit but she couldn't so we just chilled that night then the next morning she took me to the airport.

When I got on the plane and finally came back to New York, I went to my grandmothers' house who lived in Brooklyn were I stayed with my grandmother, my brother and myself in a one bedroom apartment. When I came back to live with my grandmother, I heard that in New York freebasing is not the same as in Los Angeles, here its called crack and its a whole lot cheaper than it was in Los Angeles so I started finding out where the good shit was and learning where most of the spots was. So as time went on I became what New Yorkers called a CRACKHEAD because I smoked a lot more and a lot cheaper here in New York and didn't realize that I was an addict.

I started stealing while working as a security guard where I lived which is called Marcus Garvey Housing down there in Brownsville on Rockaway Avenue and Dumont where my addition took over me. I became a monster and dangerous to myself, and those who came across my path. I hurted everyone, who ever known me for the last twenty-one years because I started inhaling this cunning cloud of smoke that became my worst nightmare. It was like if you ever watched the sitcom called "CHARMS" you would have seen that when the demons come into one of the mouth. So when I inhaled this cloud o f smoke that became my demon and until this day that same demon has conquered a lot of sick and suffering children of god that are still out there possessed with that demon.

But I, myself today which is 12-26-2009 have been clean for the past five years due to my past drug addition that led me to this point of writing this book. So what I'm trying to say is that I'm clean but now let's get back to the book at hand. My drug and my addiction led down a road that would led to my brother getting killed and mother dying three years after my brother's death which pyscology turned me into a fuckin nut and I didn't even know it now you have to understand that I smoked crack for every situation that came up every little detail in my sick thinking became a problem you name it I smoked crack behind it. Today it is called living life on life's terms back then when I began to smoke crack and became addicted they didn't have these tools so I smoked the crack like I said for any little thing that life threw at me. My mother dying, my brother getting killed all three of my uncles getting killed led me to a life of pure madness and I had no way of getting out of it until finally I went to Federal Prison for a crime that in my wildest dream I'd never thought that I could commit I mean I thought about doing it for many of years I seen it done on television on the news I seen it done in the movies but I never thought that I had the balls to do it being sober it was just a thought but once I got that cloud of smoke in me that I like to call a demon it opened up the gates of hell in my mind. I've been smoking it for about 20-25 years or more but this particular day it led me to my worst nightmare but in the long run it was my rescue.

So what I'm talking about the crime that I committed and that crime some people only imagine doing some people never met or will ever meet a person that did what I did the people that knew me and those that just met me and knows the type of person that I am was in fuckin shock to find out that I was capable of doing such a violent crime. But in my eyes it wasn't violent but in the Feds eyes it was a violent crime so what am I talking about I'm talking about something that many are called to but few have the guts to do anyone can do it man or woman and that is Bank Robbery yes! Robbing a bank was my crime. I never thought that I would rob a bank that demon took me inside the belly of the beast that I mention at the beginning of the book in smoked crack for so many years to where's I lost touch of reality I had no idea what the fuck was going on in the world. I was like a newborn baby walking outside for the first time whenever I smoked the crack not realizing that everyday I went out to find my drugs along that path I was finding all kinds of trouble that I brought upon myself, like stealing from people, lying, and bullshiting the drug dealers when all the time I was bullshiting myself.

I got so far in debt with these drug dealers until they wanted to kill me, which I didn't give a fuck, but when they threaten to kill some of the people that I loved. I made up my mind on May 7, 2004 to go rob a bank and I did it. I also got away with it and that in itself was a high that I never ever thought that I would enjoy. I'm not saying this to glorify what I did I'm just telling you the feelin that I got when I got away with robbing my first bank make no mistake about it what I did was wrong, but my back was against the wall, because my loved ones lives were on the line for some stupid shit that I did which was getting credit from the drug dealers, but that s not the dumbest shit I did the dumbest shit I did was picking up a drug that was more powerful than me so I continued robbing banks which became a second job for me and I liked it as long as I was getting away with it and getting high. But let's go back to the first bank robbery the first bank I robbed was Fleet Bank on 4-19-2004, which was in Manhattan? When I arrived in Manhattan I had no idea which bank I was going to rob there were so many banks on this one particular block. Now I must've gotten to Manhattan about twelve o'clock I think I was on Broadway and I was hungry so I walked down Broadway about ten blocks looking in bank windows to see which particular bank didn't have bullet proof glass because I haven't been in a bank in about thirty years so I had no idea on what the fuck I was doing or how to rob a bank I was just a fuckin crack head in a world of suits and ties.

Here my dirty stinking ass stepping out in some funky ass jeans that had not been washed in about nine months. I had on some fucked up thirty-dollar payless fake ass timberlands and a dingy ass plaid shirt walking around in Manhattan trying to fit in looking like a dam fool. I mean I was hungry I was fucked up I was stinking, my skin was so dark I mean I looked a total mess but I didn't care to me I looked good so with that I had to go into character and I've been told that I'm a hell' a actor, but like most drug addicts that I know we are some of the best liars in the world. So I walked my ass down Broadway with my crack head held up high and I walked my ass right into McDonald's and started begging for some food and the manager told me to get the fuck out his store in so many words.

So I did but I didn't go too far. I walked right out the front door and stayed there opening the doors for the customers. Then I started asking them can they spare some money or some food because I was hungry. Two customers came through the door a man and a woman I asked the man can he spare some change or buy me some food, he said no then the woman came and I just straight told her Ms. I'm hungry can you please buy me something to eat. She asked me what I wanted I told her and she brought it. I thanked her went back inside McDonald's and ate my food. When I finished eating it was about 2:30pm I sat there and took my time eating and thinking about what bank to rob because remember I had not been in a bank in about 25 years. So I had no idea what time the banks close, I actually thought they closed at 3:00pm. So I saw Fleet bank I went inside still carrying a bag from McDonalds' I got on the line I started to look around as I'm waiting to get to the teller I saw the teller that I wanted to serve me. I got on her line I passed her the note. She read the note as she's reading the note I looked around looking crazy as hell in the face trying to get into character for this shit because I practiced it the night before about ten times in the mirror. So basically you could say I had a bullshit plan and it was working not to my surprise because everything that I did criminally I planned it and I always got away with it but this shit here was a little bit out of my league.

I was like a fish out of water standing up there calling myself robbing a fuckin bank. All kinds of shit was going through my head when I passed her the note you see because my thoughts were not her thoughts and my thoughts was so fucked up. I didn't know whether to walk out or stay my emotions was like a firecracker. I just went off and the sparkles are flying all over the place. I was scared but I also knew I had to be calm and act like I knew what I was doing. She took the note and then backed up behind a petition so I couldn't see her for about 15 seconds. I had no idea what the fuck she was doing so I asked myself should I leave? And myself answered and said yes my feet must've heard the conversation and started trembling and shaking as if it was telling me let's go. The I looked down and saw them shaking so I said let's go to my feet then just as I turned my body in the direction of the door, I saw the teller arm reach out then my hands said wait see because I'm a little bit crazy so my girl tells me and you see I have body parts that talks to me and I didn't realize it until I was clean and sober. I mean my hands, my feet, my tongue, and my favorite one my dick they all talk to me when they want something and the crazy part is I listen to them.

Them that particular day my hands wouldn't move from the tellers window which made me look back as I was trying to walk away then I noticed that the bank teller was getting the note back from someone, then I heard a voice say give it to him, then the whole body stopped in its tracks and sort of caught back up with my hands. Then it registered with me that we were about to get some money so the teller came back to the window then started passing me stacks of money like according to the note. I couldn't believe it. I mean my brain was like all coming together then I said to myself oh shit! She passing me the money then I started reaching for the money and put it in the McDonald's bag. Then when I was that she had gave me all that I asked for, I walked away as I'm walking away I looked back and noticed that she was still passing me money. But I didn't go back to get it. I had to make it to that door which seems to me like it was ten blocks away. When in reality it was only about ten feet away.

I made it threw the door when I got outside, I realized that I was right at the corner so I made a left then I started skipping down the street while running at the same time acting as if I was haling down a cab. When in reality I was running as far away from the bank as possible. It worked I skipped for about two blocks hollering taxi! Taxi! When I got to the end of the two blocks I saw the subway so I ran down there with my 31 McDonald's bag full of money. Now normally when I take the subway I'm use to jumping the train stile. So that's what I was about to do. I got to the train stile and was about to jump over when I put my hands on the stile ready to jump I realized that I had the McDonald's bag full of money. Then I said to myself what are you doing, stupid? You got money you just robbed a bank.

Chapter 8

As I turned around to pay my fare, I saw a cop coming down the stairs on my left as the transit booth clerk passed me my metro card, my knees started shaking I looked over at the cop and he was coming towards me and staring at me as I was staring back at him. I got the feelin as I did when I was passing the bank teller the note. Something was telling me to run as the cop got closer and closer to me but I didn't listen and I'm glad that I didn't because as the cop got right up on me I saw his face expression change his mouth came open then he said to me good morning. At first I didn't hear good morning I was so scared I thought he said get against the wall but then at the back of the word good morning I heard what he really said and he said a totally different word which was how are you doing? See I was so fuckin paranoid I heard in my sick thinking everything he didn't say because remember now smoking that crack you hear anything and everything. I mean you could hear somebody spitting on the ground three blocks away when you smoking crack, so what I'm trying to say is how fuckin scared and how sick my thinking was.

When the cop approached me it's like I was in a trance when I saw him coming down the stairs but then I snapped out of it then I responded back to him and said how you doing. I did a Wendy Williams on his ass then I kindly turned around and paid my fare. Then I got on the nearest train going anywhere when I got on the train I sat in a two-seater. Then I noticed an older guy sat right next to me and kept staring at my McDonald's bag full of money. Now I knew he didn't know what was in the bag, but my sick thinking told me that he was a Detective, so when the train stopped at the next stop before the doors closed I calmly got my ass up and got off the train before the doors closed. I then went upstairs and flagged down a cab to take me back into Brooklyn. When I arrived in Brooklyn I walked to Hoyt and Schmerhorn Street and caught the A train to Broadway Junction. Now Hoyt and Schmerhorn Street has a police station down in the subway, so I had to stand there to wait for the train with transit police all over the station. So I was scareder than a black man surrounded by the KKK.

Finally the train came and I got off at my destination once again there's a police station at Broadway junction and again I was scared as I walked up the stairs to the street. Before I could get to the street I saw about six cops standing in front of Broadway Junction station, I tried not to give them eye contact in fear of one of them calling me over to them. So I kept my eyes on my McDonald's bag. I acted as if I was looking for a hamburger or fries. As I nervously walked passed those six cops once I got passed them I made a left into the park. Then I found a bench where I could sit down and look at my money and that's what I did. I sat my ass down on the bench by myself then I took a deep breath then reality hit me then I said to my self oh shit! L.A. you just robbed a fuckin bank and got away with it and that shit felt good. I mean it was a feeling that crack cocaine could not give me. I thought I was the fuckin man. Then I owed the drug dealer then I put that aside in my pocket. Then I also counted some money for my crack. I then got up off the bench walked to the store a block away from my house.

Now I owed the drug dealer fifteen hundred dollars. So I went into the store got a six-pack of Heinekens and a pack of Newport. I opened up one beer in the store and started drinking it getting my thoughts together, then I called the drug dealer that I owed and told him to come to the store and that I have his money. I also told him to bring me six movies; now movies, are a word used to say bring me six dimes. So I waited at the store for him to arrive, which took about five minutes. Now before I hung up with him I told him when he comes to get his money that his money would be in one of the bags of Heinekens and for him to dig in the bag and pull out the separate bag that had one Heineken in it with his money and to drop the six movies in my bag. So when he came he couldn't believe that I had all of his money. So he did as I asked him to do. Then he said to me you got all my money. Then I said to him yes I do. Then I slowly counted some of the money. Now I get money on the first of the month and he knew that it was nowhere near the first so he asked me where did I get the money from? My first reaction was none of your fuckin business. That's what was on my mind and that's what I wanted to say to him, but I realized the type of person that I was dealing with so as I'm thinking what to say to him I realized that the lottery board was up so it popped into my head to tell him you hit the number. So that's what flew out of my mouth, I said I hit a number then he asked me what number? Then I said to him don't worry about it you got your money right.

Now I was dying to get back to my house, but first I had to go to get me some brand new stems to smoke my crack and about two blocks away on Atlantic and pleasant, there's a gas station that sells crack pipes so I think I bought about four pipes. Then I walked back to my house. Now that particular day it was a nice sunny day and all the noisy motherfuckers was out. Now everybody on the block knew that I was a crack head and I didn't give a motherfuck but in the beginning when I first moved on that block I tried to keep a low profile, but if you're a crack smoker like I was you know that eventually this shit tells on you but as time went on I started not giving a fuck who knew on that particular day like I said I didn't give a flying fuck. I kindly walked up about four steps anxious to get upstairs I couldn't get my keys out quick enough. I knew I had just robbed a bank and I had these six movies (dimes) on me.

So I then opened the front door walked in the building slowly turned around as I was closing the door. It seemed like the whole dam block was staring at me and they really was and before I closed that door I looked around to see who was exactly looking at me. I put up five fingers then I slowly brought down four fingers leaving my middle finger up as to say Fuck y'all. Then I went up stairs pulled out my crack pipes and adjust them to my satisfaction. Then I opened up my crack all six of them poured them out on my glass table in a pile. Then I took two stems I sucked up some crack as if it was a straw then I pulled out my lighter and yes it was a Bic lighter and I took a pull off one of those pipes I had so much crack in there that the shit almost stopped my heart. Bells-n- shit started ringing off in my head. My vision got blurry; I dropped that pipe slowly now and started flying through that house. My heart must've been beaten about five hundred beeps a minute I was fucked up. Then I realized that I was too high then I ran to the bathroom and started shitting because my nerves were shot after I finished shitting I went and drank another Heineken to try to calm down. Then slowly but surely my thoughts started coming back I realized that I had put too much crack in that pipe. So then I started respecting the pipe and I took little pulls now remember I still had another pipe packed with crack that I never ever touched.

I was scared of that shit then my doorbell rang at first I ignored it but it wouldn't stop ringing. Then I went to the front window and peeped out I realized that the drug dealer had sent his flunky over to my hours, which was a female and she was not about to go away until I answered her. I didn't want to open the window because I knew everyone would look up at my window. So I went down stairs to answer the door. Then she said to me John wants to know, are you alright. Do you need anything? Then I said to her yes I'm ok, tell him I don't need nothing; I'm good now that shit was blowin my high. I was already paranoid from taken a mega blast on top of that I had just robbed a fuckin bank. So she left and I ran up the stairs back to my apartment to the window to see where she was going. She went right back over to John and I could see him looking over at my building.

Now everybody knew that he was a fuckin drug dealer so that really made me uncomfortable. So I calmed down and I made up my mind that I was going to Pitkin Avenue. I needed some new clothes. So I got my shit together and I called a cab my phone was still in so as I waited for the cab to come that crack was calling me but I knew that I could not take another hit until I finish buying me some clothes. All of a sudden my phone rang I'm thinking it's the cab company, but it wasn't it was John the drug dealer asking me if I wanted some more crack. Now I just told this flunky no and here he comes ringing my got dam phone. So I realized that, I needed to get the fuck up out of here now.

So I got my bag of money and I hid it. I took about five hundred dollars and I went downstairs I made up my mind that I wasn't waiting for that cab. So I walked to Eastern Parkway and Fulton Street then I caught a cab to Pitkin Avenue. I brought me two pairs of jeans, underwear's, a pair of timberland boots, a leather jacket, and a leather baseball cap. I had told the cab driver to wait for me and he did. After I finished my shopping I told the cab driver to take me back to Eastern Parkway and Atlantic

Avenue then I got out the cab told the cab driver to wait for me I went up in another crack spot where they had the good shit. I told the cab driver I had to drop some money off to my sister. So I went into the crack building then I realized that there was nothing but women waiting in the line to get their crack. The line was long, about ten people waiting to buy crack. Then the drug dealer saw me on the line and said to me, what's up L.A.? How many do you want? I told him I wanted ten nickels then he said here come on fuck them you're a good customer. So I started walking up the stairs to the front of the line as I started walking pass the people in line the women started grabbing my legs and saying to me, what's up baby? Whatcha doing tonite? Can I hang out with you?

I ignored them and passed my money to the crack dealer. I gave him a fifty-dollar bill then he counted off twelve nickels and I said to him I only wanted ten. Then he said to me I know but you're a good customer and I'm giving you two extra. Then I said oh ok and started walking back down stairs. As I'm walking down I seen two girls that I wanted to be with then. I said to them come with me then they said to me wait, wait I got to get my shit. Then I said to them fuck that come on I got enough for all of us. So they came with me in the cab. We went back to my house. I got a card from the cab driver with his number before I got out. I said to him come back to my house in about a hour and a half and beep the horn. I want to go to the Galaxy Hotel.

Then the girls and I went upstairs went inside my house, I told them to sit down in the kitchen then they asked me can they get a hit. I gave them both a nickel apiece while they smoked I was washing my ass. Now when you have money and crack and two women that really don't know each other they are going to try to out do each other. One is gonna do whatever I need her to do better than the other, and I realized what was going on so I came out of the bathroom back naked and started washing up in front of them. Then I said to both of them were not staying here were going to a hotel the Galaxy. I also explain to the both of them what I wanted from then and all I could hear from them was ok, no problem. Now when I get high I get generous so I said to them don't worry I'm going to take care of yall just take care of me. So I started putting on my clothes then I realized that there bitches had shifty eyes, but I kept them in one room which was the kitchen and I brung my clothes to the kitchen and I got dressed in there with them.

Then I started watching them closely to see which one was eager to please me, and which one was trying to get what she could from me and I knew that once I get to smoking that shit I'm vulnerable. So I didn't smoke at all. The greedy one for crack I got rid of her but before I got rid of her I had to see what her head game was like. So I told her to suck my dick and she did then I stopped her then I told the other one to give me some head then I compared who was better and I found out that the first one was better. Then the calm one then I asked them to pull their pants down to let me see the pussy and the ass. The calm one had a better body then the first one. Now by then I had about twenty minutes before the cab came back. So I had to make a decision quick. Now the one that gave good head I wanted to keep, but the calm one that had the pretty body had my attention, because when I smoke crack my nasty ass like to eat pussy.

So I gave the good dick sucker two nickels and twenty dollars. So she didn't feel bad then I sent on her way. Now I have about fine more minutes before the cab arrives. Now its just the calm one and I, I don't remember her name, but I'm going to call her fat pussy cause as I can remember she had a fat meaty good eat in pussy. So the cab came went downstairs got in the cab then we went to the Galaxy Hotel, but before we went to the hotel I stopped at Popeye's Chicken. I ordered a family meal then I went to the store got two six packs of Heinekens and another pack of Newports. My mind was made up that I was gonna stay there for the whole night. Then we went across the street to the Galaxy Hotel. I rented a room with the Jacuzzi. We went upstairs. I had brought some incense. I had about five more hundred dollars on me; I didn't bring all my money with me.

Chapter 9

We got to the room I told her to take a shower. While she was in the shower I got undress, I took my money and put it in my socks and kept my socks on while she was still in the shower I took a hit from the pipe that I had smoked from earlier and once I took that hit I wanted to eat some pussy. So I went into the bathroom and she was just getting out of the shower, I started kissing her and rubbing her titties. Then I stopped I went back in the room and told her to stay right there. Then I got the stem that was full of crack I gave it to her and I told her to take a pull while I eat her pussy. Then she did while she was pulling my nasty ass was sucking her pussy and then I looked up at her to see which was she enjoying more me eating her pussy or her smoking the crack. I realized that she enjoying me eating her pussy. That turned me on even more she held the pipe in her hand and lift her legs up even higher. Then I said to her let's go in the bedroom. We went into the bedroom I turned the TV to the sex channel and she started sucking my dick. Then I realized that she was holdin back when she was at my house. She sucked my dick much better than the other one. She had me climbing the walls she made me cum like that.

After I came I started eating her pussy some more. I was determined to make her cum and she did. After she came we ate some food and smoked some more crack and she started giving me some more head. My dick got hard then we started fuckin, I couldn't cum but the dick stayed hard I rammed my seven inch dick up in her like she was the last piece of pussy I fucked for a long time because I knew that eventually my ass would either be dead or in prison for the bank robbery. Then I said to myself fuck it I'm gonna eat and fuck this pussy like there's no tomorrow, eventually I got tired then we went to sleep and all of o sudden out of nowhere she started suckin my dick again by then it was about two in the morning.

Then I told her to stop and let's enjoy the crack. We smoked until about five in the morning. Then I ate her pussy some more then we fell asleep again. I then woke up and realized it's about one in the afternoon by then I'm tired of her. I had about eight crack bags left. I gave her three, two dimes and a nickel. Then I sent her on her way, I also gave her thirty dollars then she left and I went back to sleep again. The next day I woke up I went on Mother Gaston and Sutter Avenue. It was about 8am in the morning, I saw this girl with some spandex on and I wasn't sure if she got high or not so she went into the hardware store.

I had about five hundred dollars on me or more I don't remember. She was in the store trying to buy a lock that cost about one hundred dollars and she only had fifty dollars on her. She didn't have enough for the lock so I offered to buy it for her. She asked me was I serious as she went walking out the door of the hardware store. I said yes but she kept on walking. She then went into a grocery store to cash in lottery ticket so she really didn't need my money for the lock. I realized she had a fat ass and she wasn't a crack head. So I propositioned her, told her that I'll give her a hundred dollars if she'd let me eat her pussy. Again she asked me was I serious. I told her yes I am serious. So I pulled out my money and showed it to her as she kept on walking and then she asked where would we go? I told he to my room in East New York. So she asked me did I know where to get some weed, because she couldn't find any? I told her that I have weed at my house and a joint on me now. So she said ok let's go.

So we caught a cab to my house. She asked me in the cab, you just want to eat my pussy, right? I said yes so the cab took us to Crescent Street. We got out the cab. I pulled out my joint, I told her we couldn't smoke in the apartment so we took a few pulls then we went into my room. Then she asked could she use the bathroom to wash up. I gave her a washcloth to wash up, she came back out sat on my bed pulled her pants down and I started eating her pussy, while jerking off. She started Cumming, as I was getting hard then I asked her if I could have some pussy? She said no, you said you just wanted to eat my pussy. I offered her another fifty bucks. She still said no, maybe the next time. Then she asked me what kind of work you do? I told her that I rob banks. She thought I was kidding. I told her that I was serious then she got dressed. We then caught the J Train back to Broadway Junction. Then she gave me her number and told me to call her later. She got off the train at Broadway Junction; I stayed on the train to the next stop because I knew at Broadway Junction there was a police station. Then I went on the other side of the track to catch the train back towards my house. I went home and went to sleep. I woke up that night and went looking for more pussy. I found some and I went to her place and spent up most of my money with her.

Then I left went back to the crack house brought me three nickels and then called my so called girl and started crying because I knew that the police was closing in on me. I told her that I was in trouble and that I had robbed some banks and that I was going to prison if they catch me. I asked her would she be there for me. She said yes, where are you? Little did I know that she was setting me up, so I told her that I was on Herkimer and waited on the corner to see if my feelings were right. I stayed there for about ten minutes then I went to the LIRR into the tunnel to smoke up the rest of my crack. It was about three in the morning when I finished. Then I went back to the phone booth to call her and ask her could I come see her and she said yes by then I was broke, so I caught the train form Rockaway and Fulton to Nostrand and Fulton Street.

She lived two blocks away on Pacific between Nostrand and New York Avenues. I walked down Pacific Street and I found a pay phone, then I called her and told her that I was across the street from her building and to please come outside. She said ok. She lived on the first floor with her daughter. She took too long to come out so I walked back to the corner to call her. Now her daughter said that she's coming out, she's putting on her sneakers. So then I walked back down the block to the abandoned building that I was waiting in front of but I could see someone peeking out of her window not realizing because I was so high that she was setting me up. So she finally came out and started looking up and down the block then I called her and told her that I was over across the street but she said, come over here. So I did, I sat down on the stoop with her and I started crying as I tried to explain to her what I had done. I realized that she was ignoring me then all of a sudden a car pulled up by the abandon building where I was standing. Two white guys jumped out and ran over to the abandon building, a guy was walking down the street and when he got close to the building the cops grabbed him then they let him go. Then they walked back over to their car them my girl hit me on my arm to distract me from looking at the police and what they were doing. Then all of a sudden out of nowhere they came running over with their guns drawn on me. I still had a beer in my hand and they told me to stand up then I did and they told me to put my hands behind my back and I said for what? A dam beer, then they said say shut the fuck up and put my hands behind my back and they handcuffed me, they went into my back pocket pulled out my wallet, looked at my I.D. then said, yeah that's him. Then I looked at my girl and said you bitch you set me up. Then the cop told her to take a fuckin walk. As they walked me to the police car they put me in the car and I said to them all this for a beer.

As I slowly turned around too see what my girl was doing. She was standing there watching me then they took me to the 77th. Precinct. As they were booking me they took me to the front desk and I asked the sergeant at the desk why am I locked up for a beer? Shouldn't I have gotten a ticket? Then out of nowhere coops started coming around me put me looking at me. Then the cops that arrested me put me into a cell by myself. Then a female officer came to my cell holding a newspaper then she said to me yup its you.

As I was still in denial for getting caught for my bank robberies I'm still thinking that in there for a beer even though everyone in the precinct knew that I was in there for bank robbery. I'm standing in my cell like a dam fool. Still waiting for my ticket for the beer. Then one of my arresting officers came to me and said take off your jacket and your hat. Then I did then before I could sit down the other arresting officer came to my cell with foot shackles and put them on me. Then they both left thee room.

Now after drinking beer all day you know I had to piss, I was in a cell all by myself again so I started calling out to a officer asking him to let me use the bathroom, then I also asked him, why do they have shackles on my feet, but he had on answer for me as he took me to the bathroom. As we started walking again cops were starting at me. We went to the bathroom after I used the bathroom we started walking back to my cell I could see the desk sergeant, then I asked him could he please take these shackles off of me. He said to me sure, wait until the captain leaves. My dumb ass believed him as I started walking back to my cell then I sat down and waited about twenty minutes before I had to piss again. The same thing happened to the bathroom then back to my cell the cops kept coming back there looking at me. Then I asked did the captain leave yet? The officer answered no not, yell chill out as he started laughing in my fuckin face. See to them I was a fuckin joke and as I looked back I was but getting back on track I'm sitting in my cell then all of a sudden two trench coat whit guys came to my cell asked me to stand up then I asked them, what's going on? Again asking them, all this for a beer? They ignored me and then took the shackles off of me took me to the front desk to pick up my belongings the captain was not there but that ticket for my beer was.

So the sergeant kindly passed it to me saying here's your ticket for your beer. The trench coat motherfuckers put me in the car and started driving towards downtown Brooklyn. One of the cops in the car started asking me where is the money? I answered, what money? Then he said to me, oh! You don't want to play stupid. Then I said to him I don't know what you're talking about. I'm in here for a beer. Still in denial so we drove downtown now we all know that central booking is 120 Schmerhorn Street and they drove right passed it and I asked them where are we going? You passed central booking but I got no answer. Then I realized that we were headed towards the Brooklyn Bridge going to Manhattan. Then reality hit my ass. Then I said to myself oh shit, nigga you going to jail. So we went to One Police Plaza and I'm gonna cut threw the chase.

Chapter 10

They took me upstairs inside of One Police Plaza took off one handcuff then handcuffed me to a bar where I sat down. Then they started questioning me about the bank robberies that I allegedly did because I wasn't telling on myself. They had to prove that shit so I dept on denying the bank robberies. Then they started playing good cop bad cop, but that shit didn't work on me. Then I said to the good cop are you crazy? I ain't no bank robber, I'm a crack head. Do I look like a bank robber? Then the good cop asked me, what do a bank robber look like? Then I said to him what the fuck you mean, what do a bank robber look like? Shit he looks like you cause it dam sure ain't me. So then they pulled out a picture of me when I was younger then the cop asked me who is this? Then I said that's me and I looked so good in that picture. Then the cop asked, who is L. A.? I said I don't know. Then the officer's captain came in the room, he had a newspaper in his hand and he was will dressed then he looked at the newspaper then he said to the two officers good job. Then they thanked him then they unhand cuffed me and took me into the finger printing room. They fingerprinted my whole hand front, back, and the sides. And when I say they finger printed my whole hand I mean just that. The after that they took me to court 225 Cadman Plaza. Then I realized that these guys were the F.B.I. yeah I'm a little slow, because the brain was fried.

They took me down in a cell with all kinds of criminals. I mean the best of the best were there.

Then my lawyer came and asked me what was my name. Then I told her. Then I went before your majesty. Then she started asking me questions like so I understand why I'm here. Now I have never been in a courtroom like that everyone in there was well dressed and the courtroom was fly. To make a long story short my ass was going to prison. So I started crying like a little bitch as the judge started asking me where do I live? I told her I lived in a shelter on Bedford and Atlantic Avenue. I also told her that I'm not the person who they say that I am and can she let me go on my own recognize.

Then she said to me I can't let you go because you have no real residence. Then they took me back to the cell with all the hardcore criminals with one difference these criminals were rich and I was the poorest thing in there. I was clean because I had brought new clothes but I was dirty because I was smoking crack in the LIRR tunnels and I looked like a crack head in spite of me having clean clothes then we all went to a place called MDC (Metropolitan Detention Center) now I have never been in a place like this I had no idea what I was up against. I was scared, I was broke and I had burned up all my bridges with my friends. I had and I can count on my one hand about five people to whom I thought might be there for me.

Now keep in mind that I had been smoking crack for about twenty-five years straight. So I looked and I smelled like a crack head and when I say I smelled like a crack head, my breath smelled like twenty-five years of backed up shit and I found that out while I was in prison, because as time went on I started accumulating some friends and they would say to me DAM OT your breath smell like shit. But there wasn't much I could do about that at that time. I mean I brushed and goggled thinking that it would go away because when I was in the streets I wasn't taking care of myself as good as I should have. The crack had taken over my body mentally as well as physically. Then about fourteen months sitting in MDC going back and forth to court one day I went to the dentist told him about my breath and is there anything he could give me. Then he said, no. Then I told him somebody told me you could give me a pill and it will go away. I think I have gingivitis. Then he asked me so I floss? I said, no. Then he said to me then you need to start. So I did I got a pair of my pants and took the thread out of them stuck it between my teeth then started flossing my teeth and man oh man the stink and the food that came from between my teeth the shit was so bad that I wanted to vomit, but as time went on my friends were not telling me as much that my breath smell like shit but it sill was stinkin but not that bad.

Now its so much shit that happened to me in the course of me sitting up in MDC for fourteen months I dam near killed myself doing a back flip. W wind up getting about twenty stitches I also winded up in the hole, better known as the box for doing the back flip. Its not that I couldn't do the back flip because I took up gymnastic and martial arts. It's just that when I did the back flip and landed on my feet my legs collapsed because I was practicing my martial arts and I was sparing with a friend. So o was tired from fighting but I thought I had the strength enough to do the back flip and when I did it my lets collapsed because I was so weak.

I spent thirty days in the hole because I was under investigation. I was so ducked up that the prison officials thought that I had gotten into a fight. While under investigation I tried telling them the truth, but they didn't want to hear that shit. So they wouldn't let me out the box until the investigation was finished. Finally one day my cell mate said to me in order for you to get out of the box you gonna have to go hard. Now I never been in the before so I asked him what do you mean by going hard? He said, you need to speak to the captain when he comes around now while you're in the box you have all kinds of inmates and convicts that don't give a fuck about being in the box or whether or not they get out. So they do all kinds of shit up there like when a female correctional officer comes by to do her count they pull their dick out and curse her out and make all kinds of noise through out the night and ain't shit nobody can do about it because a lot of them are doing life and they don't give a fuck.

Now one day the captain and the warden was making their rounds and I was sleep, my cellie woke me up and told me yo! L.A. don't you want to get out of here? I said yeah why? What's up? He said the captain is on the floor making his rounds. So I jumped off the top bunk and ran to the front door of my cell. I saw a man-walking pass I didn't know that he was the warden. So I called him over to my cell then I asked him are you the captain? He said no. Then I said to him get the fuck out of here. Then I want to speak to the captain then my cellie said to me yo! Are you fuckin stupid that's the warden. Then I said to him motherfucker you told me to speak to the captain and he said to me you stupid ass you might have blown your chance to get out of here today. So then I started calling the warden back. Then I started apologizing, basically I was kissing ass and the warden said no you want to speak to the captain you told me to get the fuck out of here so he kept on walking then the captain came by and totally ignored me and I felt like a asshole. I then went back and climbed on my bed and all I could hear was my cellie telling me how stupid I was, rubbing that shit in.

Now the hole is shaped like a horseshoe, when they make their rounds they come in one way and go out the other way but God was on my side that day when they got to one end of the hall the other side was closed. So they had to come back my way I jumped off my bed and ran to my door then I saw the warden again talking about kissing ass I was good at it. When the warden got to my door I said warden, warden, I'm sorry I told you to get the fuck out of here I didn't know that you were, who you were please listen to me. Then he said to me are you sure you want to talk to me? I said to him yes. Then he said to me because a minute ago you said you wanted to talk to the captain. Then again I apologized to him. Then he asked how can I help you? Then I said to him I did a back flip and bust my head and it was proven to be true and I was told that I would be getting out of the box today. Then he said I heard about you that was you they were talking about. Then he said to me don't worry about it you have my word you'll be getting out today. Then he called the captain over to write down my name and number and to make sure that I got out today.

The captain took my name and number then said to me you'll be out of here by 2pm and I thanked the warden again went and got back on my bed. Now if you're not out of there by 2pm, which is the last release time you can forget it until tomorrow 2pm. The correction officer on that floor was calling out names and they didn't call mines. So I asked the C.O. I'm I on the go backlist? And she said no. Then I asked her why not? The warden promised me that I would be getting out of the box today. Then she said, oh well you're not on the list what do you want me to do? Then I asked her can you go up front and find out what's going on her response told me that she really didn't give a fuck because it was time for her to go home.

Then I turned around and asked my cellie what do I do now? Then he said to me if you want to get out today you're going to really have to go hard. Then I asked like what? What do you mean? Then he said to me when its time for them to feed us at 4:30pm after you finish eating and they come around to collect the trays don't give it to them. Their going to get angry because now you're fucking up the flow of things and you're going to become a problem. So when that time came I did what my cellie told me to do and he was right I was a problem then the C.O. tried to convince me to give up my tray, but it didn't work. I said to him fuck stat shit let me speak to a lieutenant. Then about five minutes later the lieutenant came to my cell and asked me what was the problem. Then I told him what the warden had promised me. The he said to me well if the warden promised you this then its going to happen, please give me your tray. Then I said to him fuck that shit go call the warden or the captain then I'll give you my tray. Then he said ok I'm going to call right now and when I come back if the warden said it then we will let you out you have my word and I said ok. Then about twenty minutes later the lieutenant came back to my cell and said to me pack it up Mr. Thomas you're going back to your dorm. Then I said for real, you're not bullshiting me are you. Then he said no, I'm not. I gave you my word then I packed up my sheets gave them my tray and I waited until about another twenty minutes the they came to get me, but before they came to get me I fell in my knees and prayed and thanked God for my cellie, who told me what to do. Then they took me to the front desk told the C.O. who I was then they had me to take off my orange khaki's and gave me some beige khaki's.

Now while I was walking to the elevator I could hear the inmates on my floor screaming out my name in praises saying yo, L.A. you my motherfuckerin nigga, you went hard yo! We like that shit if some of us get out we want to get with you, you aint no joke nigga you went hard, but don't come back up here man cause you know this aint no place to be, cause if you come back up here we gonna fuck you up and that shit made me feel good.

Then I got on the elevator, got off on my floor which was the sixth floor the C.O. escorted me to my dorm and everybody that were in there was so glad to see me because they didn't know what happened to me. I had lost so much blood that they thought that I had died. It was one hundred and twenty inmates in my dorm and they all welcomed me with open arms they made me feel like a celebrity. One month later after being released from the box I realized that I still was facing some serious time and that my behavior would lead to more time if I didn't change my way of thinking. So I started getting into positive programs for when the time comes for me to be sentenced.

I knew that I could not go before my federal Judge Sterling Johnson with bullshit. I had to educate myself, because judge Sterling Johnson is a fair, but a no tolerance judge. Due to these positive programs I learned sign language, which I have a certificate in as well as several other certificates that I had accomplished, such as drug treatment, certificate, life skills certificate, bible study certificate, free mason certificate and several mire that led me to better myself and to become a better man.

I was sentenced to fifty-one months in federal prison and while doing my time I got in touch with a cousin of mine who told me that my grandmother was very sick and needed my help and that she's in a nursing home and that herself is too old to take care of my grandmother and that I needed to not get into any trouble so that I may come home at my designated time so that I can fight to get my grandmother out of the nursing home. so with that in mind I knew that I ha to do all that I can so that I do not fuck up my release date, because my grandmother and my cousin was depending on me to get my grandmother out, you see while I was doing time in a federal prison, my grandmother was doing time metaphorically speaking in a nursing home. So I knew that I had to get my shit together and I focused on staying positive and with the help of my good friend and brother John Hamilton, I accomplished what I needed to do and that was to keep my head close to God, because without God and my friend Majestic I don't think that I would have made it out of the belly of the beast alive.

After serving my fifty-one months in federal prison, I came home and I accomplished getting my grandmother out of the nursing home and I now have power of attorney for her and her well being. Now you would think after all the shit that I've been through and being home for two years that w would have learned from my mistakes and teachings, but no I had toe nerve to go to the store for someone to buy a bag of weed. Coming out of the weed spot I got busted and rearrested for a marijuana charge, which led me to home confinement for four months and let me tell you home confinement can be a motherfucker.

Look forward to my sequel and get ready readers for the shit that comes next.

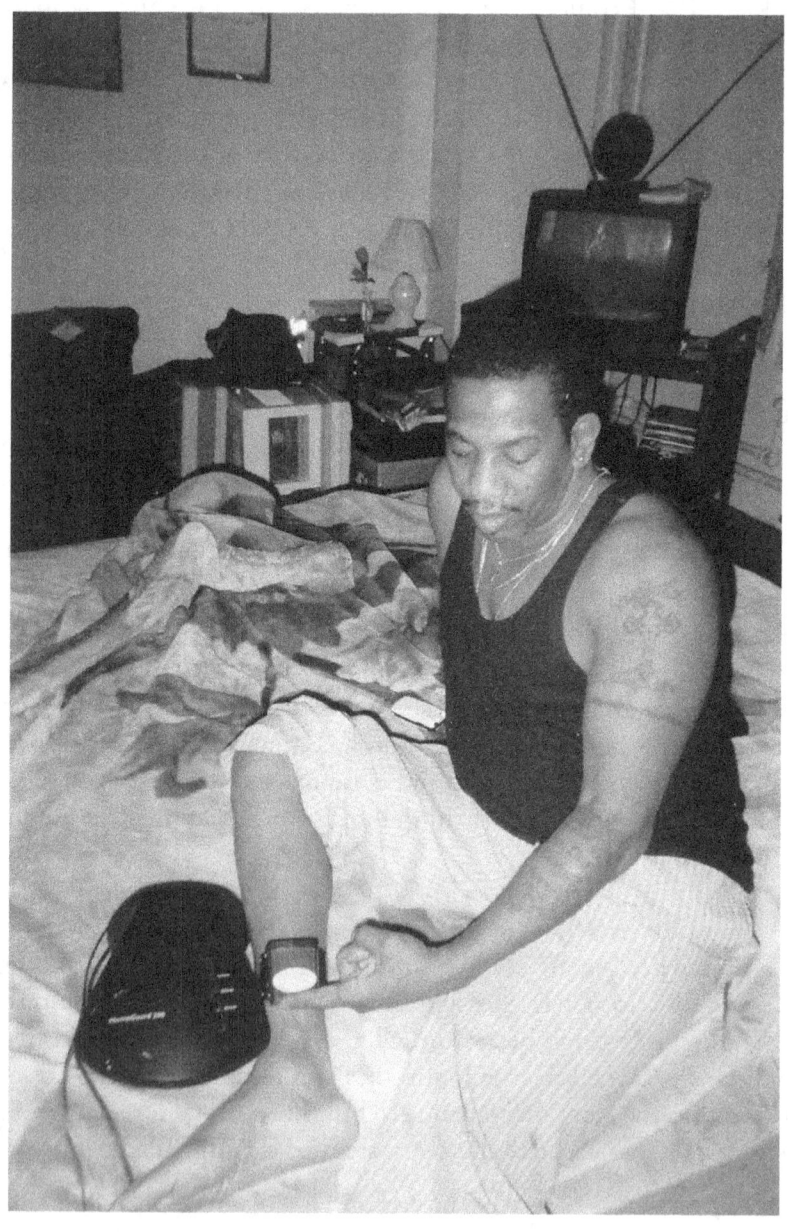

www.ingramcontent.com/pod-product-compliance
Lightning Source LLC
Chambersburg PA
CBHW060647290526
45793CB00001B/434